FOAL

WHITE WATER!

True Stories of Extreme Adventures!

Brenna Maloney

NATIONAL GEOGRAPHIC

WASHINGTON, D.C.

Since 1888, the National Geographic Society has
funded more than 12,000 research, exploration, and
preservation projects around the world. The Society
receives funds from National Geographic Partners,
LLC, funded in part by your purchase. A portion of
the proceeds from this book supports this vital work.
To learn more, visit natgeo.com/info.

NATIONAL GEOGRAPHIC and Yellow Border
Design are trademarks of the National Geographic
Society, used under license.

For more information, visit nationalgeographic.com,
call 1-800-647-5463, or write to the following address:

National Geographic Partners
1145 17th Street N.W.
Washington, D.C. 20036-4688 U.S.A.

Visit us online at nationalgeographic.com/books

For librarians and teachers: ngchildrensbooks.org

More for kids from National Geographic:
kids.nationalgeographic.com

For information about special discounts for bulk
purchases, please contact National Geographic Books
Special Sales: specialsales@natgeo.com

For rights or permissions inquiries, please contact
National Geographic Books Subsidiary Rights:
bookrights@natgeo.com

Art directed by Sanjida Rashid
Designed by Ruth Ann Thompson

National Geographic supports K–12
educators with ELA Common Core
Resources. Visit natgeoed.org/
commoncore for more information.

Trade paperback ISBN: 978-1-4263-2822-0
Reinforced library binding ISBN: 978-1-4263-2823-7

Printed in China
17/RRDS/1

Table of CONTENTS

Todd Wells is followed by two of his teammates as they explore the Chitina River.

RIVER OF RISK

The team rests in a patch of cottongrass after scouting the first portion of the Headwaters Canyon.

Chapter 1

SCOUTING THE RIVER

Alaska, U.S.A.

Todd Wells was wide-awake. Around him, his teammates snored and mumbled in their sleep. But not Todd. As expedition leader, he had too much on his mind. He had led other expeditions before, but none like this one. Todd and his five teammates were about to try something that no one had ever done before. And it was risky.

Todd's group was camped in the heart of the Wrangell (sounds like RANG-guhl) Mountains. Their tents were nestled in one of Alaska's most breathtaking valleys. But they weren't here to camp. They were here to run the Chitina (CHIT-nuh) River.

"Running" the river means traveling down it in kayaks (sounds like KY-yaks). All six team members were experienced kayakers. Yet this 130-mile (209-km)-long river is unique.

Lower parts of the Chitina River are a favorite among boaters, who take to the river in kayaks, rafts, canoes, and other small boats. But one section of the river had never been run. That's because until recently, this section was covered in ice.

The source of the river—called the headwaters—comes from the towering Logan Glacier (sounds like GLAY-shur). This massive block of ice flows into the river from the east. The Chugach (sounds like CHOO-gach) Mountains lie to the south. The Wrangells are to the north. A deep canyon cuts between these ranges, and the Chitina runs through the canyon. The first 10 miles (16 km) of the river have always been frozen and impassable.

Over time, changes in the climate have brought about warmer temperatures. The Logan Glacier has been slowly but steadily melting. As a result, this ice has become turbulent (sounds like TUR-byuh-lent), fast-moving water. Is it passable? That's what Todd and his team had come to discover.

For more than a year, the team had been planning this expedition. They had pored over topographic (sounds like top-uh-GRAF-ik) maps and satellite (sounds like SAT-uh-lite) images of the river. They had talked to local people who had grown up in the area and knew the river well. They talked to other kayakers and boaters who had paddled the lower sections of the river. They had done their homework. But now that they were here, Todd knew he needed to read the river with his own eyes. The best way to do that was from the sky.

After his restless night, Todd asked a local bush pilot to take him up in his small plane. The plane lifted off from a runway in McCarthy, an end-of-the-road town in the Wrangell–St. Elias National Park.

It easily carried them above the Logan Glacier and over the Headwaters Canyon. For the first time, Todd could see clearly what they had been studying. But he wasn't ready for what he saw.

It wasn't like looking at a map or a photo. This river moved. A lot. The gray, murky water churned. To Todd, it seemed like a living, breathing beast.

The scale of the river overwhelmed him. It was massive. In the photos, some features had looked small and easy. In real life, they were very different. He saw waves towering 10 feet (3 m) high or taller. There were deadly pour-overs, where shallow water moved quickly over partially submerged (sounds like suhb-MURJD) rocks. From upstream, these looked like big, rounded waves. But Todd knew that once a paddler got over one, he could get caught in the swirling water.

The pilot flew over the river several times so that Todd could make sense of what he was seeing. The sheer volume of water worried Todd. It was early August and unusually hot. All that heat was causing more glacier melt, which was raising the levels of the river. *Too much melt,* Todd thought. *The conditions aren't good. They aren't safe.*

The pilot flew on. There was a specific point in the river he wanted Todd to see. It was a rapid they called "the Pinch."

The Logan Glacier

Glaciers are huge masses of ice that "flow" like very slow rivers. They form over hundreds of years where fallen snow compresses (sounds like kuhm-PRESS-ez) and turns into ice. Glaciers form the largest reservoir (sounds like REZ-er-vwahr) of freshwater on the planet. In fact, they store 75 percent of the world's freshwater! Warmer weather has led to faster melting of the Logan Glacier. In the past 40 years, it has shrunk by 40 percent.

The Pinch came at the end of a 10-mile (16-km) stretch of the river. It was the biggest challenge they would face. Here, the river narrowed, and the water squeezed through a gap in the canyon walls. Todd knew there were some large, jagged rocks at the mouth of the Pinch, but from the air he couldn't see them. The water levels were so high, and the water was moving so forcefully, that the rocks were hidden. If the kayakers couldn't see the rocks, they would not be able to steer clear of them.

Todd had a difficult decision to make. Were the timing and conditions right for this expedition? That evening, he and the team held a meeting. Together, they decided that the risks were too great. They would have to postpone the trip until the weather cooled and the water levels dropped.

During the wait, Todd had another problem to solve. How would the team get their kayaks to the river? They couldn't carry them. The distance was too far and the location too remote. He could think of only one way—by air.

Finally the time came. Each 9-foot (3-m)-long, 50-pound (23-kg) kayak was strapped to the bottom of the plane and flown, one by one, to the starting point.

Todd was eager to see the river again, so he went first. When he and the pilot flew over the Pinch, Todd's stomach tightened. The water levels had not dropped. The river raged as it had before.

Three of Todd's teammates pass a horsetail falls within the Headwaters Canyon.

Chapter 2

RUNNING THE RIVER

Todd sat on a sandbar near the source of the Chitina. Behind him, melting water trickled off the Logan Glacier. He was waiting for the pilot to fly his teammates and their kayaks to the starting point. He had made the decision: The team would attempt to run the river. Now, as Todd waited for them to arrive, he worried if he had made the right choice.

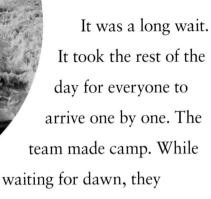

It was a long wait. It took the rest of the day for everyone to arrive one by one. The team made camp. While waiting for dawn, they planned their approach on the river. They would split up into two groups. Both groups would scout sections of the river from the safety of the high canyon walls. For each segment, they would ask the same questions: What were the dangers? Was there a safe line, a clear path? Where could they safely stop and regroup?

Next, one group would go down and run a section of the river. The other group would stay on the rocks to be lookouts and to film and photograph. When the first group was done, the groups would switch places. The first group would be lookouts now, and the second group would run the river.

There was a nervous energy the next morning as the team suited up. Each kayaker wore a thick "dry suit" to keep warm, a life jacket, and a helmet.

It took more than an hour to scout the first section of the river. Moving along the slick and icy rim of the canyon wasn't easy, nor was making sense of the chaos below. The team quickly understood that once they put their kayaks in the river, the river would be in charge. The water at their point of entry churned like a boiling cauldron. But looks can be deceiving.

The icy water took Todd's breath away even with his dry suit on. All the nervous energy disappeared. It was replaced by a steely awareness.

From the first stroke of his paddle, Todd felt the river fighting against him. Murky gray waves crashed across his chest. The water was so full of silt and debris (sounds like duh-BREE) from the glacier that he could feel its extra weight pushing against him. Reading the river was next to impossible. There was no way to see anything clearly.

The team was rapidly being swept downriver. They charged from one danger to another, avoiding rocks and strong, sucking currents. One wave would pull them underwater, and the next would force them skyward, high above the surface.

River Speak

When "reading" a river, the main features that kayakers look out for are waves, holes, and eddies (sounds like ED-eez). River waves are similar to waves in the ocean. Usually, they're safe to paddle over. Holes are recirculating (sounds like ree-SUR-kyuh-late-ing) currents. That means they fall back on themselves. Holes lie behind submerged rocks. They can be dangerous because they can trap kayakers, making it hard for them to move forward down the river. Eddies are places where the water slows down and sometimes even flows back upstream. Eddies are good places for kayakers to pull over and take a break from paddling downstream.

The sound was deafening. Their calls to each other were swallowed up by the river's roar. There was no way to be heard. The team began using hand signals to communicate with each other. From above, the scouting team watched and documented as their teammates were battered back and forth.

Todd had warned the team: Swimming is not an option. Normally, when a kayaker gets knocked out of his kayak, he swims. But on this river, that would be unwise. The current was too strong, and the rapids came one right after another, without a break. If anyone got knocked out of their boat, swimming would be hard. And Todd worried they'd be swept away before their teammates could help them.

Now, as Todd feverishly paddled, he saw a huge wave flip one of his teammates upside down. Kayakers are used to flipping. Todd knew his teammate would be skilled enough to flip himself upright without coming out of his kayak. Seconds passed before his teammate rolled up to the surface and started paddling again.

As the kayakers hurdled down the river, the river continued to change. At points, it was as wide as a football field. In other places, it narrowed. Lines of white quartz in the dark rock flashed by the kayakers like lightning.

Todd looked for a slower place where they could exit the river. He signaled to the others to follow. Wide-eyed and dripping wet, they regrouped on a rocky ledge. The river was wild, but they were running it!

Ahead, they spotted something they weren't expecting. The river flattened out for a short stretch. Beyond that lay a series of house-size boulders. At the bottom of this rapid, there were two, huge hydraulic (sounds like hye-DRAW-lik) holes, one immediately after the other. In hydraulic holes, the river rolls over enormous boulders and then recirculates (sounds like ree-SUR-kyuh-lates) upstream.

They are extremely dangerous. If a paddler were to get stuck in one, it would be like being trapped in a washing machine on the spin cycle. He might spin in his boat over and over, unable to catch a breath of air. Or, the force of the rotation could rip the paddler from his boat and send him barreling downriver.

There was no question. Todd would not risk the lives of his teammates. To avoid disaster, each boat had to be hauled up the side of the cliff by rope. Each team member carefully walked along the canyon rim, balancing his boat on his shoulders. Then each boat had to be lowered back to the river, just past the hydraulic holes.

The length of river that they were avoiding was about 1,300 feet (396 m) long. They avoided that danger, but more lay ahead: a 1.2-mile (1.9-km)-long rapid leading to the Pinch.

Todd's teammate, Matt Peters, lines up his kayak to pass through the Pinch.

Chapter 3

PATH TO THE PINCH

Before tackling any more of the Chitina, Todd and his teammates needed to rest. Atop the gray-streaked, icy canyon walls, they found the perfect spot to make camp. A series of sparkling blue pools greeted them. These were kettle ponds. They had formed where glacial ice had melted. Sediment (sounds like SED-uh-ment) settled around the ponds, trapping the water.

The water in these pools was warmer than the water in the river. Todd and his teammates dove in, washing all of the sweat, silt, and grime from their bodies. The refreshing, crystal-clear water lifted their spirits and renewed their energy.

As the sun slowly disappeared behind the mountains, they settled into their sleeping bags and looked up at the stars. They were exhausted, but happy. They had made it this far. In the morning, they would face their greatest challenge yet.

Morning came quickly. The team broke camp and began to scout the mile-long stretch to the Pinch. Early on, they discovered a deadly section of the river. Here, the river narrowed and made a steep drop. Next came a series of large boulders and hydraulic holes. The team agreed: It would be safest to carry the boats again. Luckily, the distance was only about 200 yards (183 m). The rest of the river was now theirs to run.

Todd and two other team members entered the river. Immediately, they were swept away in a brutal chain of waves. Wave after wave crashed against them. Todd frantically tried to read the river. He paddled hard to dodge all obstacles. His mind was racing: *Ferry to the left. Drive down the middle. Paddle hard. Line up to the center. Paddle, paddle, paddle.*

He was getting closer to the Pinch. There was one last group of rocks he had to avoid. He expertly guided his kayak to the right of the rocks and squeaked through the tight gap. After a mile of heavy rapids, he had made it through the Pinch.

Behind him, both of Todd's teammates had flipped, but they were fine. It had been one wild ride! But they weren't done with the Chitina yet. The team still had more than 121 miles (195 km) of river left. Most of the dangerous rapids were behind them, but what they encountered next was eerie.

The river became a maze of ice. The canyon walls took on a bluish tint as light reflected off the frozen chunks floating in the river. Navigation (sounds like nav-i-GAY-shun) became tough.

The team had to steer around drifting icebergs that were three stories tall. In places, jagged ice spires sprouted from the middle of the river.

Paddling around ice is not the same as paddling around rocks. Todd and the others noticed that the way the river ran around these frozen obstacles was different. The water created strange, powerful funnels. Everyone agreed to stay as far away from the funnels as possible. They were too unpredictable. A day passed as the team made its way through this strange landscape.

The next day, only about 60 miles (97 km) of the river remained. But with that came a new challenge: The river now broke into many thin channels. There was no high ground here to scout from. If they took the wrong fork in the river, they might end up off course and have to backtrack. Although the river was flat now, it was fast-moving. And it was so full of sediment that the water looked like chocolate milk. Paddling became a true grind. Their arms ached. The river seemed endless. And then, suddenly, they had reached the end of the river—the end of their expedition.

Todd and his teammates felt elated. They had paddled the entire Chitina River. In the true spirit of exploration, they had risked everything. And it was worth it.

Teammate
Chris Korbulic

Gearing Up

To run the river in a kayak,
Todd and his teammates needed several
pieces of essential gear. The first, of
course, is a kayak! And don't forget the
paddle. But the team also wore dry
suits, life jackets, and helmets to keep
themselves safe. And most kayakers
use a piece of gear called a skirt. This is
a piece of waterproof fabric that fits
around a kayaker and extends over the
opening of a kayak to keep water out. If
the kayak flips over and the kayaker
needs to get out, he just pulls on the
skirt and it pops off.

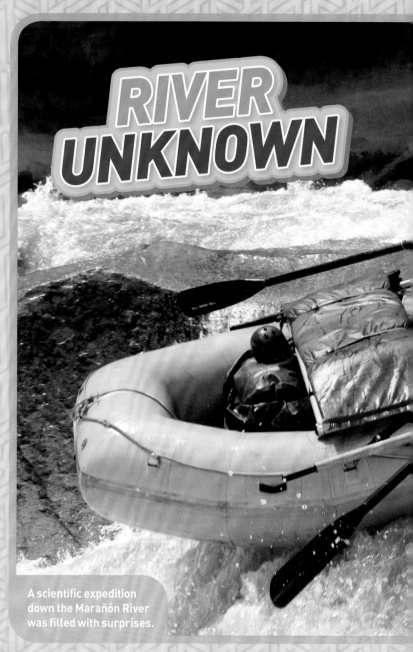

RIVER UNKNOWN

A scientific expedition down the Marañón River was filled with surprises.

The team of the Marañón Project tries to navigate through a narrow opening in the rock.

Chapter 1

Peru, South America

*B*ANG! Even over the noise of the rapids, the sound was deafening. Natalie Kramer Anderson knew what it was before she saw it. Her team was barreling down the Marañón (sounds like mah-rah-NYAWN) River. The river had narrowed, forcing their rafts through a tight, rocky chute (sounds like SHOOT).

The first boat, a cataraft (sounds like KAT-uh-RAFT), hadn't made it through. The chute was only as wide as a sliding glass door, and the current was moving fast. The boat struck one of the rocky walls. A jagged rock sliced into one of its air-filled pontoons (sounds like pon-TOONS) that kept the boat afloat.

Natalie watched as her fellow scientist, Alice Hill, fought to gain control of the now crippled raft alone. The damaged pontoon deflated, making it difficult to row and control the raft. Alice was quickly approaching the narrow chute.

Did You Know?

A cataraft is a long raft with two hollow cylinders, or pontoons, on either side.

Alice expertly fought the rapids to control the raft. She steered toward the riverbank and then hauled the raft onto land. Natalie and her teammates in the three other rafts followed. They could see that the damage to the raft was severe. The tear in the pontoon was as long as Natalie's arm.

The 15-member team had been rafting through this steep and stony canyon in Peru (sounds like Puh-ROO) on a scientific mission. They were seven days away from the nearest form of help. They couldn't go back—and they couldn't go forward without their raft, either. It carried most of their scientific gear.

At 1,056 miles (1,700 km), the Marañón is Peru's second longest river. It begins in the Peruvian Andes (sounds like Puh-ROO-vee-uhn AN-deez) and is a central source of the great Amazon River.

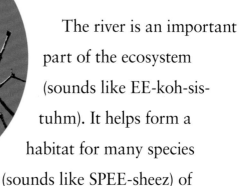

The river is an important part of the ecosystem (sounds like EE-koh-sis-tuhm). It helps form a habitat for many species (sounds like SPEE-sheez) of wildlife. People rely on this river, too.

Currently, the river is free-flowing. But that may change. As the energy demands of Peru increase, 20 dams are being planned for the river. The dams would produce electricity. But what effect would building these dams have on the people and the ecosystem?

Natalie and others want to know. They are concerned that the dams might disrupt fish migrations or change the quality of the soil. That could affect fishing and growing crops. The dams would flood cloud forest and lowland Amazon rain forest areas with water. These are spots rich in plant and animal life. Many of these plants and animals live here only, and some haven't been studied yet by scientists.

And what about the people? Would the dams force them from their homes and cause them to lose their livelihoods?

A team of scientists from five countries decided to form an expedition. Natalie and Alice became a part of this team. The goal was to study and document the river and pass on what they discovered. They wanted everyone to be informed before they made any more decisions about the dams.

But for now, the river had dealt them a serious blow. Their raft was badly damaged.

What should they do? Natalie considered their options. It didn't take long. They only had one: Fix the raft.

Luckily, the team was prepared for trouble. They had a raft repair kit. The tear was long. They would need to stitch the rubber together then use a glue to patch it.

One team member was a doctor. He had a suture (sounds like SOO-chur) kit, in case someone hurt themselves and needed stitches. He didn't expect to be using his kit on the raft!

As Natalie watched him stitching, she was reminded of her grandmother. Her grandmother was a quilter. When she sewed, she always used a specific type of stitch. Natalie wondered if the quilting stitch might work on the raft. She sat at the other end of the raft and tried a few stitches. They seemed to hold well. She tried some more.

The doctor looked up from his work. He admired Natalie's stitches. *Those might work even better than mine,* he thought.

Together, they stitched up the long tear. They next applied a type of glue that was in the repair kit. The glue would seal the tear, keeping air in and water out. They pumped the pontoon full of air and waited for the glue to dry.

Later, they gently rolled the raft back onto the river. They held their breath. Would the fix hold? It did! Now the expedition could get back under way. In another week, they would reach a resupply post where a replacement raft would be waiting for them.

Rivers, by Class

The International Scale of River Difficulty is a system used to rate the difficulty of a stretch of river. Each class reflects the technical difficulty and skill level required to navigate that section.

Class I: Easy—fast-moving water with few obstructions, small waves

Class II: Novice—rapids with wide, clear channels, rocks, and medium-size waves

Class III: Intermediate—rapids with moderate, irregular waves that may be difficult to avoid; strong eddies and powerful currents; scouting advisable

Class IV: Advanced—intense but predictable rapids; unavoidable waves, holes, or constricted passages; scouting advisable

Class V: Expert—extremely long or violent rapids; drops may contain large, unavoidable waves and holes or steep chutes with complex, demanding routes; scouting recommended

Class VI: Extreme and Exploratory Rapids—runs of this classification are rarely attempted; considered difficult, unpredictable, and dangerous

NOTE: The Marañón River was rated a Class III and Class IV river at the time of the expedition.

The white water below the falls buries the nose of Alice Hill's boat.

Chapter 2

RUSHING RAPIDS

Alice Hill knows a thing or two about rivers. She's a water resource engineer. She's also an experienced river guide. But when she helped form the Marañón expedition, she didn't think she'd be spending so much time in a "toilet bowl." That's a type of river feature. Imagine being swept up in a whirlpool where the only goal is to just *stay in the boat.*

That's where Alice found herself now. Until this point in the expedition, the Marañón had largely been a narrow, low-volume river. The team had paddled at a calm and controlled pace. All of that was about to change, though. As the river made its way through the mountains, it opened onto a junglelike section. This section was wide and fast-moving. Then the river changed again. It constricted (sounds like kuhn-STRIKT-ed) down to a thin, deep channel. Now there was a lot of water trying to push its way through a tight corridor. Looking ahead, Alice could see how the water was beginning to fold

Did You Know?

The Marañón River cuts through a canyon that in places is twice as deep as the Grand Canyon.

on top of itself, creating a series of massive, sucking whirlpools. That was bad enough, but the whirlpools seemed to appear and disappear. They would bubble up to the surface, and then sink back down.

Even if a boat got past the first whirlpool, the next boat might not be so lucky. As Alice thought about the dangers, she suddenly felt a tug on her boat. Before she knew it, she was being sucked into a whirlpool! Despite the swirling of the water and the speed of the current, Alice felt like everything was moving in slow motion.

The water lifted her boat up and turned it. She tried to predict what the river—and her boat—would do next. But she had no control. The boat spun, and then settled back to the surface of the water. Alice paddled on. As she looked behind her, other boats rose and fell into the whirlpools.

Among the team, some people were in smaller, single-person kayaks. Others, like Alice, were in larger rafts. On water like this, running the river in a kayak was like speeding down a racetrack in a sports car. But running the river in a raft was more like ambling along in a big bus. To succeed on the river, a paddler needed strength and smarts.

Alice had both. She relied on the river to do some of the work for her. To get her boat in the right place at the right time, she often looked for eddies. An eddy is an area of slower water right behind a rock. As the current splits to get around the rock, it slows a little.

Butterflies gather on a muddy bank along the river.

River Science

The Marañón River posed many technical challenges for the team. Because they were on a scientific expedition, the team needed to collect as much data as they could along the way. This meant taking frequent water samples to test the water quality. It also meant collecting a lot of insects. Why? Because the presence and abundance of bugs can also give scientists a sense of how healthy a river is.

By rowing her boat toward an eddy, she slowed her boat down, too. Sometimes the current twisted the boat for her. That was less work she had to do to get the boat into the position she needed.

When the river got too rough, the team would pull over to the side, get out of their boats, and scout ahead. It was during one scouting mission that the team discovered a deep chute with a rocky entrance.

Two team members, Robyn Scher and Chris "Sunshine" Edwards, would take a raft and be the first through the chute. They carefully plotted their approach. There were two routes they could take. The one on the left seemed a little less dangerous.

As Robyn and Sunshine made their approach, a wave carried them onto a patch of rocks. The boat hung there for a moment, and then slowly turned. Robyn and Sunshine both stood up, crouching low in the raft. They shifted their weight, trying to direct the boat. The raft slid forward, angling toward the right of the chute, not the left.

The raft teetered over the opening to the chute, and then plummeted down. All Robyn and Sunshine could do was hold on. The boat sped through the rapid and collided with a huge boulder. The impact was so strong, Robyn thought the boat had flipped over. It hadn't, but that hardly mattered. What mattered was that the raft hit with such force that it pushed Robyn and Sunshine out.

Sunshine went under. Robyn fell backward into the water but managed to grab onto part of the raft. The raft was

pulling away from her. Behind her, only the top of Sunshine's red helmet could be seen. Robyn fumbled to get her grip, but her fingers kept slipping. A massive wave struck her, tearing her away from the safety of the raft. It tumbled down the river ahead of her. She was left with nothing to hold onto. Robyn whirled around, disoriented.

Luckily, team members were stationed below the falls to help rescue any swimmers. Pedro Peña responded. Paddling against the waves, he powered over to the spot where he'd seen Sunshine's helmet. Suddenly, Sunshine's outstretched arms sprang out of the water. He grabbed onto the front of Pedro's kayak. Pedro directed his kayak toward the raft, dragging Sunshine behind.

What lay ahead was a series of Class IV rapids. This would be dangerous water for a swimmer. Pedro paddled furiously. Sunshine frantically grasped for the raft. His fingers barely caught the edge. It was enough. Sunshine hoisted himself into the raft. But Robyn was still in the river.

Dripping wet and full of adrenaline (sounds like uh-DREN-uh-lin), Sunshine took stock of the raft. One of the oarlocks, where the oar rests, had been damaged. The oar was dangling off the side of the boat, useless. He grabbed the other oar just as the boat fishtailed toward the Class IV rapids.

Robyn Scher gets soaked by a big wave.

READING THE RIVER

Robyn was still alone in the river. She fought her natural instinct to put her feet down and stand up in the water to stop herself. Doing so could be extremely dangerous. The river bottom was full of rocks. If she stood up, her feet could get wedged between rocks. She'd be trapped, and the force of the current could drag her under. She would drown in minutes.

As Robyn floated in the river, she flipped onto her stomach and began swimming. Ahead, she spotted a large rock. The water around her was fast but not too deep. She would have to make a choice: Head toward the slower water and risk getting caught in the rocks, or risk the rapids.

Going against all of her training, Robyn stood up. The swirling water came up to her chest. Fighting against the current, she staggered forward. In a few steps, she reached the rock and climbed on top. For the moment, she was safe.

Further downstream, Sunshine was in the raft, but not out of danger. He struggled with the damaged oar. Dangling from the side of the raft, it was not only useless, it was dangerous, too. He pulled it into the raft. There was no time to make a plan. Ahead, he saw the beginning of the Class IV rapids.

With only one working oar and no paddling partner, Sunshine had to battle the river alone. The sound was deafening as the raft bucked against the huge waves. His muscles burned with effort as he paddled, veering around rocks and holes.

Then suddenly, Sunshine saw movement out of the corner of his eye. Pedro was back, this time with a rope. He tossed it. Sunshine grabbed it, and Pedro paddled furiously across the river to reach the shoreline. From there, he began slowly reeling Sunshine in.

From her rocky perch, Robyn saw that her rescue was under way, too.

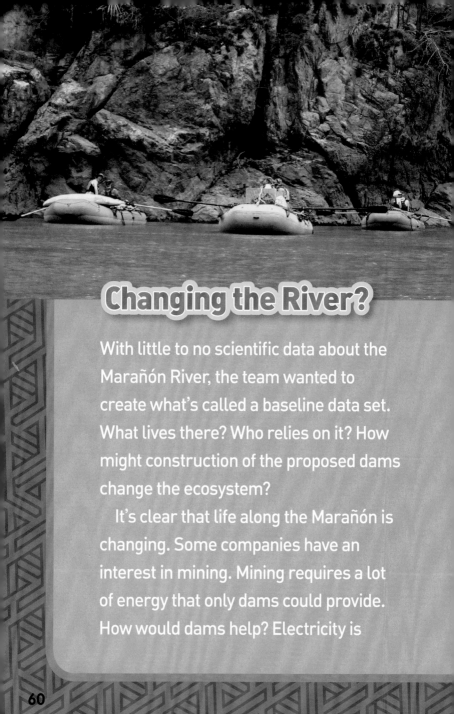

Changing the River?

With little to no scientific data about the Marañón River, the team wanted to create what's called a baseline data set. What lives there? Who relies on it? How might construction of the proposed dams change the ecosystem?

It's clear that life along the Marañón is changing. Some companies have an interest in mining. Mining requires a lot of energy that only dams could provide. How would dams help? Electricity is

produced as water passes through a dam and into a river. The more water that passes through a dam, the more energy is produced. But the team wondered if these dams could harm the environment and threaten resources—soil, water, air—that so many rely on to survive. With their data, the team created a snapshot of how the river is now. But much more data is needed to keep a watchful eye on this important river.

Teammates on the shore had finally spotted her. They tossed a rope to her, too. Robyn knew not to tie it around herself but to merely hold onto it. If something went wrong, she would need to be able to drop the rope.

With a firm grip on the rope, she slipped off of her rock, leaving its safety behind her. She flipped onto her back, keeping her feet up, while her teammates pulled her at an angle to the shore. Now she was safe. And so was Sunshine.

It took a while for everyone to regroup and recover. But soon they were all back on the river. After a time, the river quieted down.

Did You Know?

A throw bag is a key piece of safety gear. It holds a rope that can be used in a water rescue, like Robyn's.

There were fewer rapids. The water was wide and flat and calm. The team knew they were reaching a section of the river that people relied on to fish and to farm. They hoped they would meet some of these people. But they were not expecting to come across a science class!

A small group of students and their teacher were hiking from one village to another on a special field trip. The hike would take them four hours. The team offered to give them a ride instead! The students were only too happy to climb aboard the colorful rafts and meet the explorers.

As they floated downriver, the students asked many questions. But the team members asked the students even more questions. They wanted to know what it was like to live on this river. These were not the only people the team would speak to and learn from.

There were others as well. And as the expedition continued, so did their scientific research. They were documenting what animals lived in the river, especially insects. They also collected water and sediment samples along the river. This data was very important.

To determine what effect building dams or other developments would have on the river, they needed to know everything they could about the river. Very few scientific studies had been done here before, so they had a lot of questions.

How much river flow came from snow and ice? How much weathering and erosion took place? Were mining operations causing high levels of minerals and heavy metals in the water?

The team recorded as much data as they could to give them a snapshot of the people and ecosystem of the Marañón River. The more they learned, the more they realized how little they—or anyone else—really knew about the river. They also realized how special this river is. And how much it needed protection.

By sharing their data, the team hopes to inspire more expeditions and more research. They also hope to inspire a love of this river. To them, the Marañón River is worth knowing, and worth knowing well.

Steve Boyes uses a pole to push his boat down the Okavango River.

RIVER OF
DISCOVERY

When the water runs dry, the team hauls the boats through the mud.

Chapter 1

THE LONG HAUL

Angola and Botswana, Africa

Steve Boyes looked at the faces of his teammates. They were streaked with sweat and dirt. The explorers were standing calf-deep in the Okavango (sounds like oh-kuh-VANG-goh) River. The water wasn't deep enough for their boats. The only way forward was to walk, dragging the boats behind them through the mud.

This was the fifth day of hauling in Angola (sounds like ang-GOH-luh). How much more could they take? Steve knew they were at a breaking point. There was only one thing he could do. He ran.

He ran ahead to scout the river. If he could just find where the river deepened again, Steve could tell his team how much farther they would have to haul. Then they would have a solid goal and, for the first time in days, some hope.

So, he ran. He ran more than five miles (9 km) before the river became deep enough for the boats. Steve knew that at the rate they were hauling, they would need another four or five days to reach this spot. It wasn't great news, but it was the best he had. He made his way back to the team.

The team had tied the canoes, or *mokoros* (sounds like MOH-koh-rohz), together. This made hauling the wooden canoes through the shallow water easier. Not that there was anything easy about it. Each mokoro weighed more than 660 pounds (300 kg) when loaded with gear. Team members wore shoulder harnesses that were attached to the boats. Then they pulled. The work was backbreaking.

Steve's brother, Chris, paused to pick a blood-sucking leech off his ankle. Leeches were one small part of the troubles they were facing: It was hard for the team to keep their footing. There was the thick mud, of course. But the ground was uneven, too. They couldn't always spot elephant tracks, for example, before falling into one. Teammates routinely stumbled, toppling into the boats or into each other. Progress was slow and painstaking. Despite the hardship, the team was determined to follow Steve.

Steve is a conservation biologist (sounds like kon-ser-VEY-shun buy-OL-uh-jist) and a National Geographic explorer. His goal was to travel down an unexplored source river in the Angolan highlands. They would go until they reached the untouched wilderness in the center of the Okavango Delta in Botswana (sounds like bot-SWAH-nuh). The trip would take more than four months as they covered more than 1,500 miles (2,414 km).

Along the way, the team would collect data on everything they saw and heard.

That included animals, birds, fish, and insects, as well as the stories and opinions of the people who depend on these waters.

Days passed. The team hauled the boats. Deeper water, when it came, was a welcome sight. Now they could rely on their Ba'Yei (sounds like BYE-yay) teammates to help.

For thousands of years, the river people of Ba'Yei have navigated these waters. Many have perfected their skills as boatmen. A mokoro is not paddled. It is "poled." One person sits at the back of the boat and steers while the other stands toward the front,

Did You Know?

The Ngashe stick is traditionally used for poling a mokoro. This long stick is often made from the silver leaf terminalia tree.

pushing off from the river bottom with a long stick. Without obstacles, the boat glides along effortlessly.

The team had now reached a very narrow section of the river. Steve slowed his boat to a halt. The river was blocked. Large trees sprouted from the center of the river. The path forward was completely cut off. Steve and Chris climbed into the river to have a better look. The water rose to their chests. They could see no way around this obstacle. They'd have to go through it.

Teammates took turns wielding machetes (sounds like muh-SHET-eez) to hack a passageway for the boats to squeeze through. As they worked, tangled roots and branches below the waterline snagged their clothing and scraped their skin.

Okavango Delta

The Okavango Delta is Africa's last remaining wetland wilderness. It is a vast patchwork of open floodplains, simmering lagoons, sharp reed beds, and meandering channels. In 2014, the United Nations Educational, Scientific and Cultural Organization (UNESCO) named Botswana's Okavango Delta the 1,000th World Heritage site. That designation protects the delta from development. But the rivers leading to the delta remain at risk.

Those who weren't in the water chopping were searching the water for signs of crocodiles. Steve felt that the river was fighting against them, slowly breaking them down. It took weeks to get past this wild, underwater forest.

When the waterway finally widened, the team was in for another surprise. They would have missed it if they hadn't been listening. The sound of the river was starting to change. The rushing rapids were now a hollow rumbling. They didn't just hear it. They felt it in their chests. Steve gave the signal for everyone to pull over to the bank. What he saw ahead wasn't on any map.

A 26-foot (8-m)-tall waterfall cascaded over a sheer drop. The water swirled angrily around sharp rocks below. Going over the falls would mean their doom. They would have to find another way. Steve decided to "walk" the boats over the falls.

The team unloaded all the gear. Then they used ropes to lower each boat over the falls. Hours later, they had the boats and gear at the bottom of the falls, safely repacked and ready to go. As they got under way, Steve wondered what else this river had in store for them. What he wasn't expecting was to meet anyone. Yet, at the foot of the falls, the team came upon a small village.

Angola had suffered a long civil war in the 1970s. Many people fled. Bridges were destroyed, and land mines were buried in the ground to keep people from returning. These actions cut many people off from the rest of the world. No one in the village at the foot of the falls had seen an outsider before. Steve and Chris approached carefully.

As leader of the expedition, it was up to Steve to meet with the village chief. This was a great honor and responsibility. Steve wanted to show his respect to the chief and the villagers, but he did not speak their language, Luchaze (sounds like LOO-cha-zee). He did speak some Portuguese (sounds like POOR-chuh-geez). Luckily, so did one of the villagers. And so,

Did You Know?

It is not uncommon for people in this part of the world to speak several languages.

a three-way
communication was
set up. Steve spoke
and his words were
translated into the
language of the village.

Why have you come? the chief
wanted to know. *To learn,* Steve told him.
*We want to learn about this place and the
people who live here.*

The chief and the villagers showed no
fear. They were warm and welcoming.
They asked many questions about the
wider world. When the meeting ended,
the chief gave the team two chickens. It
was a generous gift. *The big world can
learn more from you than you can from it,*
Chris thought.

Hippopotamuses are a common sight in and along the Okavango River.

Chapter 2

HIPPO ATTACK!

Weeks passed, and the river began to change again. It was now about 26 feet (8 m) wide. One side was lined with tall reeds. The other side was hard riverbank. The water was murky. Steve was in the lead boat, as always. Chris was in the second boat, behind him. As Chris looked out, he saw something moving, like a wave, near the reeds.

"Something on the right," he called to Steve. "Something big on the right."

It was either something coming out of the water and going into the reeds or something leaving the reeds and going into the water. Chris couldn't tell.

"*Kwena,*" said Steve, using the Setswana word for "crocodile." Crocodiles often hang out on or near the riverbanks in shallow water. To avoid them, explorers would normally direct their boats to the middle of the river, where the water is deepest.

Chris gently called out "kwena" to the boat behind him. The call was passed back from boat to boat so that everyone would be aware.

But the animal that caused the movement in the reeds wasn't a crocodile.

And it wasn't leaving the river. It was entering it.

As Steve's mokoro approached the deepest part of the river, it rode over the back of the animal. Steve looked down and saw the enormous face of a hippo.

"*Kubu!*" Steve yelled. "Hippo!"

There was no time to react. In the next instant, the hippo lunged upward, mouth open. Its sharp tusks came down on the mokoro, puncturing the hull.

The force of impact flipped the boat over. Steve and expedition member Giles Trevethick flew over the side into the water. "Kubu! Kubu!" Everyone was shouting. Steve and Giles were in the water, but where was the hippo? Desperate to get out of the water, Steve and Giles clamored for the overturned boat. They hauled themselves onto it.

To a hippo, the biggest threat is the biggest thing. In this case, that was the mokoro. The last place Steve and Giles wanted to be was on the capsized boat. But everything was happening so fast. Both men were overcome by shock. Neither was thinking clearly. No one knew where the hippo was, but Chris feared the worst.

Chris knew he had to snap his brother out of his daze. "Swim!" he yelled. "Swim! Swim! Swim!" The sound of his brother's urgent voice was enough for Steve.

Steve and Giles dove off the mangled boat and immediately began swimming to the bank.

Know Your Hippo

The hippopotamus is one of the most feared but fascinating animals in Africa.

- Hippos can walk underwater on the bottom of a riverbed. They resurface every three to five minutes to breathe.

- Hippos secrete an oily red substance, which gave rise to the myth that they sweat blood. The liquid is actually a skin moistener and sunblock that may also provide protection against germs.

- Hippos are highly territorial and aggressive, especially in the water. They have large canine teeth that can inflict serious wounds.

Ten feet (3 m) separated Steve and Giles from safety. They dragged themselves onto the bank. That's when Chris started shouting instructions. He and another teammate poled to the middle of the river to retrieve the sinking mokoro. If they lost that boat, they were in trouble. It had precious gear on it. Some of that gear had already come loose and was floating downriver.

They hauled the damaged mokoro onto the bank. Chris leaped out and rushed over to his brother and Giles. Both were sopping wet and shaking. Their hearts were racing.

"Tea!" Chris commanded. Hot tea might help them with their shock. Chris and another teammate returned to the river to hunt down the floating gear. They searched the river for signs of the hippo.

They found nothing. They never saw it again. It may have quickly swum away after the attack.

Everyone was rattled, especially Steve and Giles. Chris had to think fast. He worried that if they waited too long to get back on the river, Steve and Giles might have trouble doing so at all.

Chris quickly made everyone busy. He asked some team members to repair the boat. He asked others to repack the gear. He stayed close to his brother and Giles.

Less than an hour after the attack, everyone was back in the boats and poling down the river. Steve was in the first position again. He would lead because he had to. Everyone looked to him. But Chris knew he had been shaken to his core.

The team poled for several hours before making camp for the night. Everyone stayed close to each other around the fire, reliving what had happened.

The next morning, Chris tried to keep to their strict routine, but there was an uneasiness in the group. They set out, but they didn't get far. Two large hippos suddenly rose up from the river, blocking their path. Only the tops of their heads were showing. The expedition came to a halt. No one wanted to push past the hippos. Steve suggested they wait it out. The hippos often settled into the deeper parts of the river by mid-morning. Steve just wanted to make sure that these two

Did You Know?

The word "hippopotamus" comes from the Greek word for "river horse"— a nod to the hippo's fondness for water.

hippos didn't see them as a threat.

The hippos resubmerged (sounds like re-suhb-MURJD). A hippo can stay underwater for five minutes without coming up for air. The team waited. The hippos rose again, in exactly the same spot. No one moved. The hippos went underwater again. No one moved.

This scene replayed itself for an hour and a half. Each time the hippos rose, Steve would say: *Just one more time*. He wanted to be sure—absolutely sure—that the hippos were not going to move. When he felt sure, Steve poled ahead, skirting the spot in the river where he knew they were. The others followed, hearts racing.

A team member uses a net to scout for fish.

Chapter 3

LAND OF PLENTY

The river has many moods. It was slow and winding as the group made its way toward the country of Namibia (sounds like nuh-MIB-ee-uh). But the river quickly changed again. This time, it straightened and took the explorers through a massive, rocky forest. The ground was carpeted with aloe plants. Soon, they found themselves poling through a tropical jungle.

Fast rapids sped their mokoros along. The team carefully navigated two short waterfalls. Then, they found themselves in a place called Mahango (sounds like MA-hang-oh). They had heard of this place before but were stunned by what they saw.

The river had brought them to an open plain. It was filled with animals as far as the eye could see. In the middle stood about a hundred hippos. Steve looked at Chris. *How are we going to get past those?* they silently wondered. But it wasn't all hippos. A herd of 60 elephants had also gathered. Baby elephants were playing in the water. The sky was alive with birds.

That night, the team began looking for a spot to make camp. That's when Giles stumbled upon an elephant-hunting camp.

Eight bushmen sat around the site. Giles thought the camp might be illegal and these men might be poachers. He quickly reported to Steve what he had seen.

Steve and Giles returned to the hunting camp. Five elephant skulls were buried with their tusks sticking out of the ground. The hunters were waiting for the skulls to rot so they could gather the valuable tusks. Elephant meat was drying in trees.

Steve spoke to the bushmen in Afrikaans (sounds like af-ri-KAHNS), a language spoken in South Africa. He learned that the men were not poachers. The camp was legal. Wealthy hunters paid for the right to shoot and kill elephants. These men worked in their camp.

Why would you do this? Steve asked.

It's a job, the men answered. *It's work.*
Steve and Giles left the camp with heavy
hearts. This was a place they wanted to
protect and preserve. They did not want
anyone shooting and killing elephants. It
was hard to sleep that night.

A few weeks passed, and the team
had crossed into Botswana. They were
approaching a place they knew well, a
place full of life. It is called Mombo.
To Steve and Chris, this place represents
everything that they are trying to protect
in Africa.

To get there, they had to cross several
difficult channels. Like the beginning of
their journey, the team found themselves
pushing and pulling the mokoros again. It
was during this time that they encountered

a herd of 20 or 30 buffalo. Cameraman Neil Gelinas had an idea. He wanted to capture an image of this herd from the air. So he launched a drone with a camera. Neil guided the drone over the herd to get a great image. And that's when the buffalo started stampeding. The wall of buffalo was only about 300 feet (91 m) away from the team. For a moment, the team stood frozen. Then they yelled.

If they ran, they'd be run over by the buffalo. Their best chance of survival was to hold their ground and make as much noise as possible. The buffalo kept coming, closer and closer. The yelling grew louder and more desperate.

Protecting the Wild

Steve and Chris Boyes have dedicated their lives to protecting and conserving Africa's wilderness. For many years, they have explored one of the world's richest wilderness areas, Botswana's Okavango Delta. Thanks to their efforts, the delta is now a protected place. But so long as the rivers that feed the delta remain unprotected, the Okavango Delta itself is at risk. The Boyes brothers hope that further exploration will help inform, inspire, and ultimately protect these wild places.

With only about 65 feet (20 m) between the explorers and the herd, the buffalo pulled up short. They changed direction, thundering past the explorers. It was another close call for the team.

They had hardly recovered from the near collision with the buffalo before thousands of birds greeted them. They had reached Mombo! Everything about this place said: Life! The river was only about 13 feet (4 m) wide here. Hippos lined the banks. There were three or four large herds of elephants.

The team wanted to stay in this paradise forever. But they still had several weeks left to travel. The goal was to reach the end of the river. The Okavango Delta is one of the world's largest inland deltas. This means that instead of ending at an ocean, this delta empties out into a desert, the Kalahari (sounds like kah-luh-HAHR-ee) Desert.

But when the moment came, they weren't ready for it. Suddenly, there was no more water. With their mokoros beached, they were standing at the edge of the desert. Chris and Steve looked at each other in disbelief. They were dirty and tired. They were cut and bruised. Their clothes were in tatters. Their muscles were raw. Could they really be done?

The team cheered and wept with joy. The journey of the river was over, but another journey was about to begin. Chris and Steve knew they had to share the story of this remarkable place to protect and preserve it for all time.

THE END

DON'T MISS!

NATIONAL GEOGRAPHIC KiDS **CHAPTERS**

DANGER ON THE MOUNTAIN!

True Stories of
Extreme
Adventures!

Gregg Treinish
with Kitson Jazynka

**Turn the page
for a sneak preview . . .**

Gregg warms himself in the sun one morning during his long hike along the Appalachian Trail.

THREE
SECONDS
OF COURAGE

Staying in the raft is one major goal on the Arkansas River in Colorado, U.S.A.!

ONE FOOT
IN FRONT OF
THE OTHER

The deep, frosty water of the Arkansas (sounds like AR-kan-saw) River churns white as it rushes over the rapids called Frog Rock. The spot can be found in the shadows of the Colorado Rocky Mountains. It's framed by huge rocks, evergreens, and—on that spring day— a low ceiling of ominous clouds.

I was trying out for a summer job as a white-water rafting guide.

Did You Know?

A rapid is a turbulent, fast-flowing, and potentially dangerous part of a river.

I had never steered a raft before, though!

Well, this would be like some of my other adventures, I told myself. I grabbed my paddle and jumped in the raft. The rushing water, mostly snowmelt from the Rockies, was cold, cold, cold.

A mile (1.6 km) or so down the river, the water curled and sprayed in huge arcs against a tumble of boulders. I misjudged the rapid. The raft hit a rock and bounced hard to the left. I flew out of the boat into the unfriendly water.

The heavy raft, still carrying my passengers, surged over me. The weight of the boat held me under in darkness. I couldn't breathe. I choked back river water. The water pulsed past me. I couldn't get to the surface.

I felt my way to the edge of the boat, trying not to panic. After what seemed like an eternity, I popped up into the air and took a ragged breath. The others reached for me. I grabbed their hands and climbed back onto the raft.

The instructor asked if I was still good to go. I coughed, wiped my face, and said, "I got this." We finished the run.

I left that day not knowing if I had the job, but that event helped me believe I could do great work in the outdoors. I had been reading a book called *A Walk in the Woods* by Bill Bryson. It's a fantastic memoir (sounds like MEM-wahr) about a man who hiked a section of the Appalachian Trail.

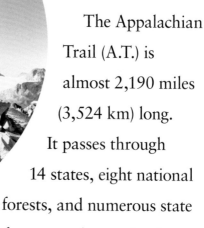

The Appalachian Trail (A.T.) is almost 2,190 miles (3,524 km) long. It passes through 14 states, eight national forests, and numerous state parks, forests, and game lands. It's a hiker's dream.

Something about that book grabbed my attention. I couldn't stop reading. When I read the last page, I knew what I wanted to do. I walked into the living room and told my roommate I was going to hike the A.T. the next spring. That's the best time to start so you finish before winter. Plus, I had a lot of preparation and planning to get through first.

As luck would have it, I got the job as a white-water rafting guide. That summer, I worked on the river three days a week. I also worked as a preschool teacher to make extra money. And I prepared for the Appalachian Trail.

I planned every detail of the hike down to the tenth of a mile. I read books about the trail and built my strength on training hikes with my backpack full of bricks and firewood. While the preschool kids napped, I plotted out where I'd resupply and exactly how far I'd walk each day.

I think the planning was a way to trick myself into believing I was ready. In reality, I was pretty inexperienced. While the A.T. is an established trail, there's no telling what your experience will be or even if you'll finish.

All the while I was preparing, my mom was worrying. She didn't like the idea of me hiking alone. She thought I'd be killed by a black bear. But I was set on going. I told her black bears rarely attack people.

In March, my parents met me in Georgia and drove me to the trailhead. Together, we hiked up Springer Mountain to the southern start. My parents were excited for me. We had a tearful goodbye.

Fifteen minutes later, I ended up back at the parking lot. It turns out, the trail north crosses south before it heads north

again. I was confused and frustrated.

I met another hiker also walking the wrong way. His name was Jamie. Together, we figured out where to begin. Jamie set off ahead. I hugged my parents again and walked off alone. I was scared and excited at the same time.

Later that day, I caught up with Jamie. We met a guy who had been walking the wrong direction for a whole day! We got him straightened out and walked together for a while.

In those first couple of days, my pack weighed 45 pounds (20.4 kg). . .

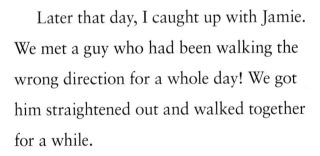

Want to know what happens next? Be sure to check out *Danger on the Mountain!* Available wherever books and ebooks are sold.

INDEX

Boldface indicates illustrations.

MORE INFORMATION

To find out more information about the explorers and projects mentioned in this book, check out the links below.

The Chitina River:
mountainmindcollective.com

The Marañón River and related issues:
maranonwaterkeeper

maranonproject.org

paddlingwithpurpose.com

The Okavango River:
adventure.nationalgeographic.com/adventure/adventurers -of-the-year/2016/steve-boyes

intotheokavango.org

CREDITS

**This book is for Liam and Devin, of course.
Everything I write, I write for you.   —BM**

ACKNOWLEDGMENTS

I'd like to thank Steve and Chris Boyes, Todd Wells,
Natalie Kramer Anderson, Alice Hill, and Robyn
Scher for trusting me with their stories. I wish
I had lived them with you; I hope I told them well.
Thanks also to my editors at National Geographic,
especially Shelby Alinsky, who asked me to write
the book, and to Kathryn Williams, who faithfully
read every word. I'm grateful. Thanks to the whole
team at National Geographic.